Items should be returned on or before the last date shown below. Items not already requested by other borrowers may be renewed in person, in writing or by telephone. To renew, please quote the number on the barcode label. To renew online a PIN is required. This can be requested at your local library.
Renew online @ **www.dublincitypubliclibraries.ie**
Fines charged for overdue items will include postage incurred in recovery. Damage to or loss of items will be charged to the borrower.

Leabharlanna Poiblí Chathair Bhaile Átha Cliath
Dublin City Public Libraries

Baile Átha Cliath
Dublin City

Pearse Street Branch
Brainse Sráid Piarsach
Tel: 6744888 2228431

Date Due	Date Due	Date Due

Mary Turley-McGrath

OTHER ROUTES

ARLEN
HOUSE

Other Routes

is published in 2016 by
ARLEN HOUSE
42 Grange Abbey Road
Baldoyle
Dublin 13
Ireland
Phone/Fax: 353 86 8207617
Email: arlenhouse@gmail.com
arlenhouse.blogspot.com

Distributed internationally by
SYRACUSE UNIVERSITY PRESS
621 Skytop Road, Suite 110
Syracuse, NY 13244–5290
Phone: 315–443–5534/Fax: 315–443–5545
Email: supress@syr.edu

978–1–85132–114–8, paperback

Typesetting by Arlen House

Cover image: 'What Traffic' by
Bernadette Cronin (nbcroninsc@yahoo.ie)
2000, oil on canvas (17ins x 19ins),
is reproduced courtesy of the artist

CONTENTS

9   *Acknowledgements*

HERE

17   Bearings
18   The Bell Arch Date
19   Moon Gate
20   Mount Talbot House
21   Scan
23   Butterflies
24   Sycamore
25   Magheroarty Beach
28   Love Song for Winter
29   Winter in Donegal
31   Light Box
32   Spring Break
33   From the Sands
34   Two-Point-Two
35   Winter Meetings
37   Westland Row Revisited
41   At the Station
42   Holles Street
43   Blue Ginger
45   The Sea at Wicklow
46   The Black Castle
50   Points
51   Essexford
55   Eglantine Avenue
56   Triptych

THERE

61   Brighton Pier Reunion
63   Pigeons

64 Strathaven
65 Finding Cádiz
66 Mondragón's Palace
67 Castillo del Aguila
68 Sunday at Castillo del Aguila
69 Santa Iglesia Catedral Málaga
72 In Rota
73 First Night in Tel Aviv
75 Adoration of the Shepherds
77 The Astronomer's Daughter
80 Off the Lines
81 Toronto Cargoes
82 Front Street West I
83 Front Street West II

ELSEWHERE
87 Enceladus
88 Ghost Country
89 Under the Words
90 Valley of the Birches
91 Hamlet's Ghost
92 Year's End – St Stephen's Green

94 *About the Author*

for Beth

and for Eoghan, Angela, Thomas and Oisín

ACKNOWLEDGEMENTS

Thanks to my family, especially Helen and Teresa, for their help and support, and to Jim for being my first reader. My thanks and appreciation to my brother and sister-in-law, PJ and Marion, and to Aunt Teresa for continually giving me new insights into my native place. Also to Ted and Mary O'Callaghan for their knowledge of Castleknock local history. Many thanks to Annie and Martin Mooney who introduced me to the landscape of Serranía de Ronda and to Jackie and Alan Sherling for the opportunity to visit the Holy Land.

My appreciation for the critical reading and support given to my work by Errigal Writers: Denise Blake, Imelda Maguire, Averil Meehan, Patricia Morris, Clare McDonnell and Celine McGlynn; also for the support of the Rathmines Writers and the Inchicore Ledwidge Society. My thanks to Tina McGlynn and Marcella Molloy for their patient proof-reading.

A very special thanks to Nuala Ní Dhomhnaill for the Winner's Award for 'Valley of the Birches' in the Trocaire/Poetry Ireland Competition 2014, later published in the Trocaire/Poetry Ireland pamphlet. I am very grateful for the bursary to Annaghmakerrig which was part of that award.

'Holles Street' and 'Mount Talbot House' appeared in *New Roscommon Writing* 2014, and *The Roscommon Herald* (2015) respectively. 'Magheroarty Beach' was shortlisted in the Listowel Writers' Week Single Poem Competition 2014.

My thanks to all in Poetry Ireland for their encouragement and advice over the years.

To Alan Hayes and Arlen House for publishing this book, my sincere thanks.

'It must have been an endless
breathing in: between
the need to know and the need to praise
there was no seam.'

– Margaret Atwood, 'Butterfly'

OTHER ROUTES

HERE

BEARINGS

Trig points set to past, present, future,
those dots and triangles plotted in margins

once became mysterious mind-maps
to anchor my thoughts, then free them;

now I think they were phantom trajectories
charting journeys to come or already done,

like trig points on mountain tops
more rests below the surface than above.

THE BELL ARCH DATE

Even on a clear day you can barely read
the feeble numbers on the keystone.
The mason would not have known
that he had carved into limestone
the date of the blackest Famine year.

One of the strong men who shaped
stone for the twelve-foot orchard wall
from blocks blasted in Tibarney quarry,
then carted over the village bridge
and up the avenue to Thornfield House.

Dozens of hands worked these stones:
wheeled, carried, cut and chipped for
months and years till the job was done.

Then the planting started:
apple, pear, peach, fig; exotic trees
lined the south wall where an iron pipe
ran below the surface carrying steam
to warm the ground in winter.

All the trees are gone: the wall remains;
and if the soil is thin, old paths emerge
where hooves of sheep cut into clay.
There are no mosaics, no inscriptions;
just the bell arch date: 1847.

MOON GATE

This morning in the Walled Garden we linger
in the Moon Gate, cradled in its ring, soothed
by an ancient magic, standing together, arms
stretched out to the sandstone curves.
We are part of life's great wheel, blocked now
between seasons as April's east wind shears
the Herb Garden where mint, thyme, sage,
lie dormant, unready and unwilling to grow.

'Roses will blaze in summer borders', you say.
I know the fig tree will flower and fruit,
artichokes and kale will flaunt their verdure.
For now, nothing stirs; so we leave to follow
the path under oaks and beeches that shield
sea-blue anemones and old-gold daffodils.

MOUNT TALBOT HOUSE

That big house stole my soul:
drew me into its crumbling walls
through black-eyed windows

of mock-Tudor turrets that watch
like antique antennae across fields
divided by the twisting river.

It sensed my presence then
as I skirted round the barbed wire
that fences off its imploded heart

buried where roof and ceilings fell
under pouring water from roof tanks
blown up during troubled times.

The treasures of the big house lie
buried here: the grand piano,
ancestral portraits in the long gallery,

lacquered cabinets of glass and china,
and William John Talbot's volumes –
English literature, French and Greek.

A blanket of healthy ivy clings
to the westward wall and creeps
towards the massive square tower.

Who will hear when the last walls fall
in a gentle rumble some stormy day?

SCAN

I

Outside the clinic, a warm July morning
lifts my spirits. A whiff of wild woodbine
from the hedge beside the silver birches
brings me towards the garden. It was your
favourite wild flower; you brought it home
despite all those miniscule black insects.

I take three blossoms and stop to stroke
the birch trunks, smooth as velvet bone,
solid and gentle, almost human to touch.
The bark splits and unfolds in the dry air.
I strip off two pieces that curl into scrolls
of light-brown vellum marked with dashes;
is this your secret message, a print-out
of some binary code or a native design?

II

You were still alive when I came here first,
that warm day I could not relax on the couch;
the scanner whirred over me to read density
for print-outs in yellow, green, red.

Now, six years on, I close my eyes, ignore
the whirring, starting, stopping – and think
of you. They had no scans for you at sixty;
when they did check, the harm was done.

The doctors did what they could
until the morning of that third Sunday
of the new decade, your femur snapped.

'The scan is finished now', the nurse tells me,
'little change from the last time'.
But everything has changed.

BUTTERFLIES

Today I watch them again, three white butterflies
above the purple buddleia at the garden's end.

August afternoon fills my room while they revolve
in cascades of ritual flight-dance, up and down,

spiralling one another in a tremendous helix,
teasing time and space with an aerial *pas de trois*;

behind them, blackcurrant leaves wither:
whitethorn berries redden.

SYCAMORE

We killed the sycamore today, under an angry August sky
the branches swathed in wraps of lusty leaves;
no hint of autumn in stems pulsating red: only a scatter
of blackspot across its fronds like ornate pentagrams.
The roots had split the tarmac and probed foundations,
the upper branches waving higher than our house.

We were here before it came, a stray sapling I dreamed of.
It sprouted at the wall's end, the gorse bushes protecting it;
our children gave it space and didn't play there anymore.
I watched them grow, but it outstripped them and soared
as we came and went, went and came, each magic season;
its sticky-coated buds in spring, soft green leaves of May,
full-flush of green in summer, the blackspot of September
on huge brown hands sodden in winter grass under the line.

It watched us all those years, reaching out, growing taller,
its bark changing with each season; rejoiced in January days,
branches silver and strong in snow, a trunk smooth as silk.
In storms it never lost a branch, steady in southwest gales;
the trunk forked in time, made a better canopy: in summer,
mosses filled up the v-shape like a crotch.

You propped the ladder at the fork, the silver saw whirred
as a black flex trailed back for current to slice each limb.
When you lopped the biggest branches, one crashed
between the tool shed and garden kerb: the other toppled
between the black salley and gorse. All went silent.
We stood looking at the split torn bark, ripped back by
the wrench of the fall. We caressed damp cream flesh:
I counted trunk rings, just twenty-one.

MAGHEROARTY BEACH

I

Twin boats lie under blue plastic near the pier;
high above them the masthead wires vibrate.
The ensign cable rings along the hollow mast,
earthing the sound like bells at a holy place.

We go eastward along the beach, eyes slitted
against specks of creamy grains, then swerve
seaward to where sand is so packed and clamped
by the receding tide, it forms low serried mounds
moulded and patterned like the sand dunes
in aerial photographs of the Sahara.

But here there are no caravans, no camels decked
with blue and red tassels, no golden girl
on a white stallion sweeping her hero to Tír na nÓg.
Two figures move towards a jeep at the sand's end.

II

The dunes slope higher. We cross a scatter of stones,
each granite ball curved by relentless scouring tides.
From here the beach stretches out into a crescent
of creamy-brown, the colour of over-ripened wheat.

Waves roll long and low with milky crests;
further out the water is turquoise, then dark green.
It deepens to grey and black towards the horizon
of ink-blue clouds, the kind of ink mixed in a beige
and brown earthenware bottle in school
and poured into white inkwells by the Master.

Black and blue fuse in this sky arching from the point
of the beach, across Inishbofin with its monastery ruins
and sea-caves of seals and over Inishdooey and Inishbhig,
fixing itself further west on the bulk of Tory Island.

III

Seabirds drop like dive-bombers to catch their prey.
These missiles of feather disappear below the water,
re-appear and fly on. The seals feed further out,
then vanish from sight. Knots of smaller birds skim low.

When evening comes, we have walked only half the beach;
we leave the point for another day and turn toward the pier.
The wind has changed; it whips squirts of sand into our faces.
Over Tory, the rays of a Jacob's ladder reach for earth.
I pull my hat over my eyes and scan the beach
in a wine-red glow through the loose stitching.

A flock of gulls screams where the stones are scattered.
I pick three stones, granite eggs, speckled black and silver
in the palms of my hands. I give you one as a keepsake.
You left that autumn; they are all that remain with me now.

LOVE SONG FOR WINTER

Leaves
on the bog road rolled
into copper swathes under stretching beeches,

in a maize-yellow coverlet of sycamore palmates
near the graveyard gate,

in dabs of translucent carmine
where the sun glances over a confusion of brambles.

No leaves on the blackthorn,
just bare spikes spearing the morning sky.

WINTER IN DONEGAL

There's something about December Sundays –
morning silence, more silent,
the stillness, even stiller,
clear air, clearer
than at any other time of year.

Something hopeful begins
with trumpet fanfares on the radio.
Then rain and hailstones strike,
bouncing off the concrete path.
Thousands of minute pellets
wipe the last of autumn's colour;
yellowed-green of black salley,
silver birch's golden hearts.

How different from last Sunday
when all was still and lucid,
we walked Rathmullan beach.
The tide was so far out
I felt it could never return.
We stopped at a chunk of driftwood,
then doubled back.

At the pier a fishing boat unloaded
crates of prawns; fishermen watched
them weighed into smaller boxes
for the huge freezer truck.
The boat was emptied except for
five crates of *scad* stacked on the deck.

A young fisherman standing there
looked up at the Sunday crowd.
He glanced at the dismal deck,
then at his miserable overalls.

Did he feel the call of the landlubber's life
as the fingernails of winter scraped his bones?

LIGHT BOX

Life's great peace lies in winter afternoons –
December sunlight pours onto open pages,
its angled beams make a light box on my table,
penetrate the paper, illuminate black on white,
recast words and lines, then drive the shadow
of my pen across the page by select solar force.

If I remained here long enough, I would change
into a new being, a creature of bioluminescence,
transformed by cosmic pulses to a new dimension.
Sunlight, maker of strong bone, waker of bones!

SPRING BREAK

We stop for fresh air at the Esso station
and Tim Horton's coffee in the dark red paper cup –
a tonic in the sunshine after our three hour drive.

We take a stroll and look across the flat land
to Sligo Bay. A narrow road twists from the station
along the coast; cars emerge from behind tall reeds.

At the side of the station two young fellows go berserk
washing their cars: radios blare as they drag blue hoses
over bonnets; the suds skids over glass and alloy wheels.

As if from another world my poet friend appears.
He has survived another winter in his house by the sea
watching beloved barnacle geese cross from island
to mainland. He tells me he saw a white hare in the snow.

We exchange news and books, then go our opposite ways.

FROM THE SANDS

A sound I had not heard before

like the swish of a Victorian skirt
or the gossip of tiny dry leaves;
around us they floated, ribbons
of sand-grains, gliding, dipping;
undulated by southwest winds
along the length of the beach.

Was it dark matter made visible,
that unknown part of the Universe
revealed; or the part of ourselves
we do not know, as we search for
the perfect time, place or person,
that endless seeking for what is?

The sand-grains mimicked the sea's
rise and fall at a hand's height;
we walked with them and dared
not turn, till at last we ran to the dunes.

A sound I never heard since.

TWO-POINT-TWO

it rated on the Richter scale;
high for a Donegal earthquake,
strong enough to make a loud rumble
on a January night

so that you sat up
in bed thinking a car had crashed
at the corner and ripped in under
the old pines and hawthorns.

I missed it all in my quiet city bed,
although at some stage in the night
there was a thud;

perhaps a book
had fallen from a shelf or the rattle
from the baby's pram we missed
on our walk to Blanchardstown next day.

An earthquake struck there too –
over a hundred years ago –
when the old monastery was shaken

and the monks rushed to the chapel,
prayed day and night until the morning
a white blackbird sang in the orchard garden

and sang there for weeks, like he belonged
and had found
a home among the winter trees.

WINTER MEETINGS

I met you on a damp afternoon in the same café we met
    before.
We talked, you cried and told me of your plans to leave
    the city.
You left me with a gift wrapped in Christmas paper.
'A small book of poems', you said, 'translated from the
    Russian'.

Darkness hung over the Liffey, the bus windows fogged up.
Behind me two schoolboys discussed their project;
how to throw an egg into the air so that it returns
    unbroken.
'I have a book of drawings and inventions',
the dark-haired boy said, 'I want to be an architect'.
'Cool', the other replied, 'I'd love to see them sometime'.

I imagined them on Sundays in the park, fitting eggs
into all sorts of contraptions; their mothers furious when
omelettes had to be made and all the eggs were gone.

Two young Chinese men sat across the aisle. They chatted
in perfect English, then switched to Chinese.
The African girl in front of me, wrapped in a cream jacket,
hummed and tapped on the silver handrail like on a piano.

Shopping bags cluttered the aisle and schoolbags lay
    under seats;
Christmas lights threw gaudy reflections on our shoulders.
I struggled down the winding steps, past the cardboard
box on the corner step with the bones of chicken wings
left as an offering to the god of plenty.

Later, I unwrapped your Christmas gift, the slim book of
    poems,

the pages gone yellow – the kind I like;
Yevtushenko's 'Zima Junction' begins:
'As we get older we get honester,
 that's something.'

WESTLAND ROW REVISITED

I

This was where I first arrived –
the train's strong heartbeat overhead
is the only thing that seems the same,
its iambic rhythms rock and fade.

The railway bridge spans
the lunchtime traffic like a giant
chocolate bar on six columns;
tiny pages of caked dust peel

from these pedestals to pavements
stained by star-shaped vomit traces,
peppered with chewing gum
and flattened cigarette butts.

The red-brick houses that stood
opposite the station are gone.
Even the birthplace of Oscar Wilde
cannot be entered from the street.

II

The world inside Trinity College walls
was then a *culchie, keep out* zone.
I followed the high black railings
to D'Olier Street for the Rathmines bus.

I longed for a life inside
those grubby granite walls
and the frail curtained windows
in need of painting.

III

Today in autumn weather
small knots of people leave the station:
older men with briefcases, young men
with computers, girls with shoulder bags.

I have no ticket, I cannot revisit
the platform for the Westport train.
Other awkward *westies*, full of hope
and energy, cross that platform now.

They are coming in over this
and other bridges in the autumn sun.
This station brought me here,
it does not want me back.

IV

I bless myself at Saint Andrew's Church;
in Viking times a Danish temple
to Thor and Fregjia stood here
outside the city walls.

Past the Spar shop and Café Sol,
I turn into Lincoln Place. At last
this season I have found my place
inside the college walls.

I can take my time, stroll
across the cobbled Front Square
towards the blue-faced clock –
then out under the triumphal arch.

AT THE STATION

You did not see me as you left the platform,
turned through the swivel gate and crossed the road –
the safety barrier still down.

I called your name and the wind blew words back
into me. I gained pace until I was almost parallel,
the lines of speeding cars between us now.

I did not call again but watched your coat blow back,
your left hand resting on your stomach, head bowed
as if talking to the baby inside.

You were never so close to me, never so far away:
like in the film of *Dr Zhivago,* in the final frames
we see their love-child for the last time:

a plain business-like girl with a headscarf,
quite unromantic in herself, who hurries home
with her young man, a balalaika on her shoulder.

I saw the film my first weekend in college.
I still remember that sunlight through winter trees,
Julie Christie's hair, Omar Sharif's gaze, love's despair,

as if here I could never cross this road to hug you
or that we would walk forever in parallel lines
like the railway tracks in the film, glinting, stretching.

HOLLES STREET

You sleep in the see-through hospital cot,
milk drunk after the midday feed;
I delight in your newfound ease outside
the womb you stretched in for weeks
while we watched the tracery of your fists
and heels, signs of strength and growth.

Outside, on Merrion Square, artists fix
their paintings to the Sunday railings:
a kaleidoscope of shades on black bars
overhung by summer-heavy trees.

I lift you up, crane my neck to allow
your three-day-old eyes see beyond
open double windows, the world
awaiting you, where I may not belong.

BLUE GINGER

Summer came
as it often does in mid-September,
and on the Square, flower baskets hang
over ice-cream vans, kids holding hands
and tired young fathers pushing prams
beside their awkward pregnant wives,
watching others with lonesome eyes.

Underneath the cream umbrellas
nimble waiters wave silver trays
against their all black shirts and ties;
their sallow skin and gorgeous eyes
more suited to *bellissimo* or *buenos días.*
But never mind, we have them here
in tight pants and soft leather shoes.

Only God knows how you regret
the days their dads revved up their cars
belting around by the Colosseo,
speeding like Apollos in convertibles.
While from the sea the evening breeze
comes cold against your skin and hair
and evening shows you what is what,
who remains and who will not.

Up past St Michael's jutting steeple,
where right above the entrance door
the miserable dragon lies all impaled,
the Town Hall clock watches it all.
Outside the Blue Ginger Restaurant
you read the names of tasty dishes:
Creamy Pasta Carbonara, Salad Caprese,
Hereford Steaks on lava stone.

So back you wander to your hotel
for peace and quiet, to rest your head
from women's talk of this and that,
ailing husbands, their demanding brats.
You get a phone call from himself,
sounds quite exhausted, fixing presses.
Ah well, you told him not to bother
and draw the curtains for the night.

The extractor fan below the window
keeps purring on till after midnight.
It's booming on again at two and then
at four you're going mad. The wretched
duvet is far too heavy; you hate the things,
wish they never were invented. At last
you dream a fitful dream that summer
came in mid-September.

THE SEA AT WICKLOW

After twilight it unwinds,
pitches spray over the sea wall
against rocks lined southward
as far as the eye can follow.

The green-black waters heave
like a submarine monster.
The insurge and outsuck vibrates
ruins of the Black Castle and soaks
the twisted stone steps.

I edge along to the lighthouse wall,
count the beats of its blinking eye;
then pick my steps to harbour level,
past lifeboat sheds and clubhouse lights.

THE BLACK CASTLE

I

In our house by the sea I wake
on a bed of air and glide from between
the acorn-topped mahogany bedposts.

I merge into the presence of the room,
slide red velvet drapes across silver poles
to allow pale August light flood in.

Outside, the young sycamore offers
hand-shaped leaves in welcome.
Sea and sky are twinned in grey,
seagulls scream over the Black Castle.

Two local women, their heads close
in fresh morning gossip, traipse
towards town, handbags dangling
from their arms.

II

I leave the house and garden, cross
the road for the field that leads
to the sea. Here, a man walks his dog,
loosens the lead, then calls him back.

The field ends in a sheer drop
to rocks that are beaten and broken
into splintered pieces, jutting from
the swell like stray black teeth.

The sea's song is a hollow heaving,
a submerged moan, translated
by slap, slush, slop, re-echoed
where it wears into the rock.

Voices carry in the quiet air,
thin and light, expanded by space
like the sound of lost angels
seeking theirs hosts.

The east wall of the castle remains;
its serried stonework worn by weather
into the shape of a black-robed monk
fixed in perpetual prayer.

III

Rocks slant out against the waves
and a small beach reflects the light.
This is where St Patrick and his monks
tried to land to preach the faith.

Local people stoned them from the shore
until Patrick agreed to leave,
if only they would take from him
the injured monk

whose face and teeth were broken
by their stones. In pity, the local women
took him and nursed him back to health.
They befriended him, loved his story

of the risen Christ. To them he was
a fertility god bringing only good.
They called him Mantach – missing teeth –
and watched him pray to his wooden cross.

IV

When his strength returned he built
a hut of stone. His hands bled and
his feet blistered until boys came
to help him, bringing younger brothers.

In return he taught them healing,
not with spells and curses, but with
songs and blessed water. He brought
power to their wells, blessings on

their harvest, comfort to their sick,
health to their children.
Young men joined him; they prayed together,
wore simple robes, built more stone huts.

Yet, Mantach pined for his old companions,
kneeling each evening facing eastwards
in solemn prayer.

POINTS

Returning from the city again
summer falls
to trees and fields beyond
the Boyne where
a Jacob's ladder hangs

like that evening on the Strand
before you left
nothing to hold
onto or hope for
ever wondering if you would
or could come back even

as I try to learn the things
you had begun
lines across the page converge
to the vanishing point
we did not reach that evening

sand dunes too sharp
wind whipped grains across
the beach for a sky drama
fallen to earth mirrors
fusing us together.

ESSEXFORD
County Monaghan 1599

I

Under his jerkin,
the cold of her cross,
like the tip of a dagger
ready to thrust.

His soldiers were hungry,
uneasy, unpaid, when they
stopped by the ford
at the end of the day.

For months in this country
he knew bogs and marshes,
wretched natives in cabins
wasted by war.

Each night in his tent
he dreamed of her touch
on his cheek as he bowed –
the old ravens called.

II

Under his jerkin,
the cold of her cross,
as over the boglands
curlews were crying

to herons that woke him
with each change of watch,
by morning his fever
was worse.

O'Neill's banners were open
when dawn mists had lifted:
he called for his captains
to make terms of peace.

The swans flew east
and cloaked out the sun,
he prayed for evening
and an end to that day.

III

Under his jerkin,
the cold of her cross,
as he sailed up the Thames
none came to cheer him.

No trumpet sounded
in Her Majesty's Hall,
as if she had never
known him at all.

At the turn of her head
he was beckoned aside,
he had nothing to give her
no captives, no gold.

IV

Under his jerkin,
the cold of her cross,
as early one morning
her men came to get him.

He pleaded for mercy,
offered them riches –
the old ravens called
as he knelt at the block.

Under his jerkin,
the cold of her cross.

EGLANTINE AVENUE

Chaucer-like, I set out for Botanic Gardens
down the road of high red-brick houses,
some *For Rent* or *For Sale*, a few derelict.

Behind one grey-white tattered lace curtain,
someone has put six red tulips in a jam jar
to brighten up the world.

Further on, near the Malone Lodge Hotel,
a pigeon beats frantically
inside a top-storey window where
the lower doors and windows are boarded up.

The high bare trees are ghostly.
I cross Stranmillis Road to Botanic Gardens
and a burst of primulas at Kelvin's statue
clears the greyness.

I head for the museum entrance –
what is dead and gone is fixed
and easier to understand.

TRIPTYCH

I

Morning

Drabness fills the room, inching up from rushy fields
between the road and river. Everything is grey-green,
except the blue dredger and it stopped two days ago,
its single arm like the bent leg of a lost monster.
The fresh daub it filched from the river tops the bank;
this shone at first, now it fades to black with the wind.

Even the crows feel the brunt of winter; they resist
the gusts, drop lower or swoop towards the ground.
Some double backwards and seem to bounce about
as if pulled by an invisible thread; they call to one
another and complain. In the distance they become
faded dots like floaters in an injured eye.

II

Evening

The Continental Market at City Hall presents
the best of food and Christmas fare. An arch
at the end of Donegall Street reminds me
of the souks along the Via Dolorosa.
I remember that other city, so full of the past
a future cannot be born. Unlike this city
of red-brick facades full of new energy,
escaping the past to hold a brittle present.

In Victoria Square we take the lift to the top
where evening darkness has disappeared
beyond the glass triangles of the dome.
This new heaven mirrors the scene below:
silver balustrades become sky-ice swathes,
our waving bodies are quadrupled above us
merged with the happy students on the mall.

III

Morning

We walk from the glass arrivals hall into the warm
dry light of Málaga, then sit in the bus shelter to drink
a coffee from Gambrinus. A young woman joins us.
She wears a camel coat and has travelled from Paraguay.
She tells us that they never have snow there, only rain.
I imagine blue and yellow macaws flying for shelter.

The bus hurries through Marbella towards the station.
Christmas lights string the streets and orange trees gleam
with fruit, fabulous and full, their vibrancy filling the air.
Poinsettias pack the tiered stands on every street corner
and decorate the garden kerbs of Cerro Blanco. Here,
I can absorb light and colour through every pore.

THERE

BRIGHTON PIER REUNION

Ten years gone by;
the girls are young women visiting
the pier in their old school gang.
Pasts and presents collide
as memories flow back.
They laugh a lot, flick their hair,
smile sadly at the Turbo Coaster
and Extreme Booster at the pier's end;
then they ramble back from the edge
to the Ghost Train and Helter Skelter.

One of them drops back to look
at the Gallopers – those gaudy animals
of the merry-go-round; why does she stop?
What happened at this place, a happy day
with parents now divorced or dead,
or the scene of her first kiss?
What have these plastic creatures
– horses, chickens, lions – reminded her of?
She stands in the sunny morning breeze,
the others call, she runs to join them.

They stroll back along the boardwalk.
Underneath, the water circles and chaffs
against the struts of steel legs corroded
and encrusted at the water's will.
They watch workmen in black jackets
hammer down the timber ends,
nailing down the loosened strips.
The sea air makes their faces ruddy.
They are now in the present, heedless
of the flowing tide under slatted boards.

The laughter calms as the last friend arrives –
a toddler by her side. She pushes a young man
in a wheelchair, returned from Afghanistan,
wearing his poppy for Remembrance Day.
They embrace their friends with delight,
lift the toddler into the air, swinging bags
of shopping, Jaegar, Bravissimo, Benetton.
The sun comes out in force as they amble
back once more to the funfair of their youth.

PIGEONS

Even now I can recall their early
fretful flaps over Victorian rooftops
before traffic started.

They sound-waved the day's entry
to my half-sleeping brain
disturbed by light's quick coming
to this city by the sea,

across the confine of chimneys,
over flat-roofed stores, bike sheds
and back yard extensions with not even
space for a child's swing.

Once they stopped their flapping
I was drawn into the lungs of morning,
and wondered what their flapping means –
no bird call, no cooing, just flapping.

After breakfast, the pier's delights
were broadcast out along the coast.
I watched swimmers pass yellow buoys
on the olive-green sea, smooth as velvet.

Children screamed from the Helter Skelter
and Haunted House. The brown boats
were still tied up on the Water Ride,
suspended in space above the rills

like the brown tub-shaped boats
that I attempted at Alton Towers,
lost my nerve and had to turn back –
against a queue of people with their kids –
red-faced and embarrassed to find freedom.

STRATHAVEN

Last October in Strathaven Park,
mounds of yellow leaves lined
the base of the barbed wire fence
between the park and fields beyond.

Pinioned there in heaps, driven
by wind and rain, glued together
in their own oils, they criss-crossed
and gleamed like cloth of gold.

They would never reach the fields
that slope westward where black cattle
grazed and sheep cuddled in small knots,
their necks folded over one another.

And I think of you my friend, at peace,
looking down on this town with its narrow
bridges and racing river and North Street,
the place you loved as a young bride.

FINDING CÁDIZ

The smiling city, rising from the sea,
its golden cathedral dome and spires
on the morning horizon in December,
as we crossed the bay from Rota.

The ferry moored at the port's end
opposite the high elegant facades
of a city, old as the first seafarers
from Tyre and Sidon.

Their bloodlines still run in families
who live in narrow cobbled streets
– like Calle Antonio Lopez – darkened
by rows of tall silent houses.

It was Constitution Day: crowds filled
Plaza de Mina to eat fresh fish and bread;
the tops of palm trees vibrated
with the screams of invisible wild parrots.

In the Casa Museo I found at last
statues of Melqart, the Phoenician god.
He stands created as: merman, nature-lover,
king-like Osiris and as a replica of Baal,
the fire god who gave us *Bealtine*.

And nearby are the busts of Astarte,
Earth Mother and protector of sailors
who risked new seas in search of routes
to carry fish, wine and wheat eastward –
returning with cedar, silk and gems.

Drowned amphorae from the seabed prove
nothing is ever completely lost.

MONDRAGÓN'S PALACE

Late February in Jardines de Chefchaven,
and the fountain is still, the palace noiseless.

From the columns of the Mudéjar courtyard
we wander to the terrace above the precipice.

Rows of box hedges still smell of damp,
oranges on a single tree gleam in the sun.

Two horses, a bay and a grey, graze below us,
a child runs to drive goats towards the shed.

On the horizon
a tower in the trees watches through dark eyes.

CASTILLO DEL ÁGUILA

We saw it in the distance last year
from the narrow road that twists to Gaucín.

Far away it towered like an eagle's eyrie
watching our every move to his lair.

But we did not reach it that day –
content with the best local wine by an open fire,
laughter, gazpacho and roast lamb.

Later, we watched the Genal winding through
the valley below, overhung by carab and oak

and almond blossoms like suspended confetti
across the plain, releasing us from winter

to spring's rebirth in bursts of pink, white
and faintest red.

We looked upwards in hope; waited for eagles,
hawks or falcons to drop

from the Castillo, dive to our mirador
and carry us to the snow-capped peaks of Ronda.

SUNDAY AT CASTILLO DEL AGUILA

That Sunday we drove to the Castillo,
but first, Mass in the Church of San Sebastián
near La Ermita del Santo Nino.

We inhaled cold February air as we entered
through the high wooden door, heavy enough
to stop a charging bull.

The floor of black and white marble tiles
was beautiful but cold, so we sat
with our shoes on the kneelers keeping
our soles warm.

Our eyes wandered to the black timber roof
above round white pillars decorated
with bands of gold near the top.

The church was dark, only a few small windows
in a village that boils in summer and chills
the bones in winter.
We thanked God for the waiting sunshine.

SANTA IGLESIA CATEDRAL MÁLAGA

Two huge paintings face one another
across the sanctuary.
The High Altar soars
like a buffer between them.

I

The Banquet of the Pharisees
by Miguel Manrique
is a seventeenth century *Last Supper*.
The long white table fills the centre,
bare except for a plate of fruit.
Jesus and Mary Magdalene
are watched by dark-robed guests.

Jesus has moved forward
from His place at the head of the table.
The others have moved back
to make space for the kneeling woman.
Her dappled brown dress, spread
like faded plumage, is offset
by His flowing crimson robe.

His right heel rests in her palm,
the foot touching her dress.
She bends and kisses the place
the hem of His robe touches the shin.
Her other arm encircles His leg.
Her long hair has fallen from her neck,
the bare shoulder and upper breast
are a sigh of softness in the dim room.

The guests are transfixed,
their faces drained of colour;
they throw angry glances at the woman.
Jesus leans forward;
the power and passion are His to give
in the open hand stretched down to her.

II

The Beheading of St Paul
by Enrique Simonet – 1887,
is a study in light and blood.
Paul's severed head, encircled
by golden light, rolls towards
a group of white-robed priests.

They recoil up the white steps,
retreat into the temple's darkness,
eyes fixed on the double horror:
a haloed head and the bloody path
that trails behind the head.
From the waist-high execution pillar
the Saint's pale torso slumps,
the hands still tied with cords.

The executioner stands defiant,
body tanned and rigid, his face
holding the fury of the fatal blow.
His arms and chest are bare,
his strong legs prepared to stride.
The execution sword has fallen
onto his victim's garments.

Behind the executioner
stands a silent crowd; their sorrow
is palpable; no horror dims
their gaze of pure compassion.
An old man leans on his companion.
Roman soldiers front the throng,
their legion's eagle spears the sky
where bursts of onyx light rush in.

days seem to duplicate;
time folds back from its axis
reflecting that afternoon last year,
by the sea at Caesarea when storms
had washed over the ruins, leaving
the Crusader City cut off.

I am by the sea again, not the coast
where the Phoenicians departed,
but north of where they landed.
A ship is on the horizon. Waves roll
noisily, then calm with darkness.
Soon, beach and *paseo* are empty.

The lighthouse looms over the port,
the beacon has begun its rhythmic
on-off flash like a steady heartbeat.
Evening brings its own light:
the floodlit walls of Castillo de Luna,
candles on tables in Bar La Concha.

At the Castillo, Christmas tents sell
jams, leathers, incense, winter hats;
the tents are shaped like ice pagodas.
A huge crib holds pride of place:
no baby Jesus there as yet, just a fire
set in a corner with an artificial flame.

In Plaza de San Roque strollers gather
round the chestnut seller. Steam pours
from a tall black pipe as the nuts roast.
Families share them from paper-twists
and saunter by the Chapel of Vera Cruz
where God rests under Baroque ceilings.

FIRST NIGHT IN TEL AVIV

All day, a storm had raged across the city:
palm tree branches lined the motorway,
in Shalom Shabazi drains overflowed,
it took all my force to close the taxi door.

Rachel waited at the courtyard entrance;
she guided me up narrow cement steps
without a handrail. I prayed not to sleepwalk
and fall onto bits of plaster, empty tins
and buckets left in piles by the builders.

Inside, gales had smashed a window pane,
glass slivers sparkled across the red carpet,
but there was food in the fridge: dates, figs,
bread, milk, kosher chocolates.

My bedroom was inside the apartment door;
it let in a healthy draught from the courtyard.
I longed for a hot whiskey as I piled up
coats and jumpers on the bed.

I awoke to a strange noise in the darkness –
a man's voice, half singing, half wailing.
I remembered Rachel had pointed towards
the mosque in Old Jaffa when she said,
'you'll hear the muezzin's call to prayer'.

Early morning brought voices of children,
someone practising the piano downstairs.
I could see the minaret crescent between
the city and the sea. I was East at last

in the heart of this place that cannot
make up its mind between old and new –

solar panels on flat roofs, shiny skyscrapers
and young men in posh hotels wearing
business suits, hats and prayer shawls.

Things should have changed then,
they did not.

The Kings left – all three of them –
riding their silken-tasselled camels
into the northern horizon.
Their servants followed, a motley mob,
miserable wretches like ourselves,
half-hidden under jars of food, water
and camel fodder.

They had no time for gold, incense or myrrh,
did not value wealth, only how to use it:
they withdrew from it as a child from fire.

Our journey home began, back to the hills,
to the flocks we left unguarded.
Like men released from a spell, we grabbed
our water-skins and crooks, then stumbled
out of the cave, leaving the family behind.

Jonah, our leader cursed our foolishness:
were we duped by a host of angels?
We were not Tobias, Jacob or Moses,
angels had no business with us.

I went back to the cave one more time;
the woman was singing to her child,
the man stood by, folding her robes,
muttering about other routes to Egypt
and what his angel had told him.

I helped him fix straw into the manger;
something fell on the floor and rolled
to a corner; a gold coin shone.

'Keep it', he said, not even looking,
'we have plenty without it'.
I slipped it into my tunic pocket.

We journeyed back in deep silence,
our sandals heavy on our feet.
Stolid men, ashamed they had
been fooled by a dream,
ashamed of themselves and each other
on the hard road back
when joy is gone.

The flocks were all there
under the acacia and tamarisk trees,
not one missing.
It was the first miracle.

Things should have changed then,
but we did not.

THE ASTRONOMER'S DAUGHTER

As chief servant to the High Priest
I listen to all suppliants on days
my Master prays in the temple
or attends Pharaoh's council.
I sit in the cool of the colonnade
by marble pillars laced with vines.
From sunrise on, I listen to all,
but by temple law may speak to none.
At noon I rest in my chamber.

Sometimes I sleep and dream of Tia,
see her walk up the temple steps
or glide towards me down the colonnade.
She brings gifts from her mother's house;
a basket of figs, an amphora of new wine,
a brace of ducks netted by hunters
at evening in the river marshes.

Most wondrous of all, once she carried
an armful of irises, deep lapis lazuli.
They lasted three weeks on the white
temple altar. When they withered,
I saved a few, dried and pressed flat
under the weighty scrolls that clutter
my chamber, leaving room only
for my pallet, chair and table.

That was before sickness ravaged
the city. The rich left for the country
but the poor came each day.
The colonnade filled with the smell
of fear, the stench of their sickness.
The vines stopped growing and faded
to nothing. The pilgrims grew fewer,
the smell of fear banished by smoke.

Days passed in a haze, I grew weak.
The High Priest remained in the
inner sanctum, some say he died there.

I waited,
fed by the wisdom of the scrolls.
One day someone brought food,
water and tapers; forty days passed.
Then the storm came, it rained for days.
When it stopped, all was silent.
My strength returned, my courage grew.

The vines were torn from the colonnade,
the steps to the temple shone white
in the sun; no pilgrims, no beggars.
People returned.
The first groups carried bundles,
then came the carts and slaves
and later, horses and chariots.
I ordered the servant to prepare
my palanquin, we passed through
cleansed streets.

In the astronomer's house all shutters
were closed, the doors firmly locked.
Each day I waited, prayed to see Tia
at the end of some line of pilgrims.
Winter was ending, swallows darted
through colonnades and arches.

One sunset I heard the soft slide
of her sandals. I feared to look.
Then I did. Her eyes were light green
flecked with brown, dark wells of pity.
In her arms she carried a bunch of irises,

deep lapis lazuli. At the end of the steps,
her guards stood and waited. She said:
'Tell the High Priest my mother is dead;
I am the astronomer now, your daughter'.

OFF THE LINES

Words and letters cast shadows
on the white space
skewered by their spires, hooks and angles.

Words throw shapes to capture this world
and worlds of thought,
feelings, ideas, time past, time passing.

Words send probes into space like cathedrals,
splitting the light with ornate pinnacles
over the tomb of Columbus, seeker of new lands.

Words send depth-charges to underworlds,
like the Arctic lake two miles below the ice,
holding new lifeforms, millions of years old.

TORONTO CARGOES

In the night, trains rumble;
deep caravans of thunder
through cathedrals of echoes,
trailing out past Fort York
like invisible tails of comets.

Under Bathurst Bridge
their cylinder carriages slip slow,
red, blue, ochre; then square ones
in yellow and silver;
one day, nearly a mile long –
we counted one hundred and six.

I turn back to sleep, wondering
where they will be when light
brings the city to life again.

Once Lake Ontario reached here
before it was pushed back by drains,
ditches and landfill for roads, houses
and the railway under Bathurst Bridge;
pushed back for over a mile to where
the Waterfront and Queen's Quay banks,
bars and skyscraper blocks now stand.
Like the sea, it is ever present, but ignored.

Yet you can still see the lake:
a skinny, deep blue line on the horizon
behind the scrapers, trees and cranes.
You can see it better from the south side
of the rooftop garden, a banished thing,
abandoned, left aside like an old friend.

FRONT STREET WEST II

We explore your new home for the first time;
you the host, a reversal of parent-child roles.
Light and dust scatter over the wooden floor
as you open the balcony doors. We can study
the city below us on this early June afternoon:
the red and white streetcars on Bathurst Bridge,
its high, steel sides like rib cages that shelter
travellers entering and leaving its shaded zone.

The city began here; moats and banks repelled
natives and enemies; the defender's bones rest
under the maple leaf flags; this fertile ground
where trees are deep green after a mild winter,
their thick canopies coating the Fort York skyline
and beyond to the Gardiner Expressway and lake.

ELSEWHERE

ENCELADUS

Last night I dreamt of Enceladus
hidden by Saturn's rings,
tucked in like a love-child,

erupting in fountains of ice,
blocks, pillars, boulders of ice,
all thrown from its living gut,

some pieces falling back,
others spinning into space
sucked into Saturn's wheels,

swirling and bumping,
splitting and splintering,
spinning round and round,

their facades changing
and catching sunlight
in never-ending light.

I floated through this
tormented chaos
and the silence had

its own music
I could not understand,
but knew the meaning still.

Do not try to understand,
do not fear, it is far
beyond your realm.

GHOST COUNTRY

I was neither
Living nor dead, and I knew nothing,
Looking into the heart of light, the silence.
– T.S. Eliot, 'The Waste Land'

We never sailed those fjords before,
secured in pristine silence
by immaculate air

so maddening we wanted to shout,
shout and shout into an emptiness
that begged to be filled;

fjords, once blocked by glaciers,
opened by warmer waters, exposed
a coastline of inlets to the interior,

to the incised rocky lunar landscape
where bears roam and musk ox beat
barren ground where life under the surface
lies frozen since the last ice age;

but once cored out in tubed samples,
spores will regenerate and multiply
on a sterile petri dish.

That summer, he worked on the Reichsbahn;
his first job
to nail the broken timbers of the freight trains.

'Make sure they're empty first', his father said.
'Why?' asked Franz.
His father scowled.

Trains for the camp arrived all summer.
Through their slatted sides he glimpsed
dark exhausted faces, breathed in putrid air.
He spoke to them; no one answered.

Once he loved the tracks;
the sun's icy gleam on exquisite parallels.
Now, he felt them darken after each load
that passed under the words.

For miles before they reached the place
they could smell it; a hideous stench
that none remembered from before
when they burned towns or hamlets;
by now they knew the smell of death.
Young soldiers retched; others jeered,
then swallowed the last dregs of vodka.

At dawn they trudged towards
the line of ever-spreading smoke.
The wintry sun wore the veil
that belched endlessly so that now
there was no horizon; just a hellish pall,
even the fences were wrapped in it,
the barbed wire impossible to cross.

The creatures appeared from huts
like corpses animated by morning;
they shuffled towards the fence,
grinning weirdly, their bones ready
to split their faces, their shaven heads,
as if the skin were about to vanish,
leaving moving skulls in tattered rags.

The soldiers stopped; only a young one went on.
They stretched their bony hands to his
but he cried out remembering the day
his mother returned from the gulag.
He was six years old.
The memory that plagued him, now made real;
he fell to the ground.

HAMLET'S GHOST

Ten years have gone since I left Elsinore,
or at least that part of the play
where the Ghost speaks to Hamlet
before being dispatched too soon
by an overzealous glow-worm.

That time of year, students could still smell
shiny newness from their books
and were full of expectations.

The video kept their hopes topped up:
the classic Olivier version where once
the centre-whorl of hair on Hamlet's head
became a black and white centrifugal vortex,
years before Stanley Kubrick dreamed
2001: A Space Odyssey.

YEAR'S END – ST STEPHEN'S GREEN

The frail blue sky is unforgiving;
the sun blinds so completely
I bend my head, follow the kerb
edged with rotten leaves.

On the corner of the Green,
steps lead to a yellow door
with six nameless bells.

Thin net curtains hang still,
greyed whiteness untouched;
papers and plastic bottles pile
under basement windows.

The chime of a tram distracts,
a tuning fork note that spins
and fades down a fixed line.

Two down-and-outs slump
by the railings. One wears
a bowler hat and watches
a blackbird in the leaves.

Footsteps fall and fall;
no one stops to stare.

About the Author

Mary Turley-McGrath grew up in Mount Talbot on the Galway/Roscommon border and now lives in Letterkenny. She holds an M.Phil in Creative Writing from Trinity College Dublin and has published two collections of poetry: *New Grass under Snow* (Summer Palace Press, 2003), and *Forget the Lake* (Arlen House, 2013).

In 2014 Mary was the winner of the Poetry Ireland/Trocaire Competition; was shortlisted in the Listowel Single Poem Competition and the Cúirt Short Story Competition. She was the first recipient of the Annie Deeny Award through the Arts Council/An Chomhairle Ealaíon and The Arts Council of Northern Ireland. Her poems have appeared in: *The Irish Times, Poetry Ireland Review; The SHOp; Revival; The Roscommon Anthology 2013; The Forward Book of Poetry 2011.*

Other Routes is her third collection of poetry.